THE JOURNEY TO SOURCE

MARIA KITSIOS, LMT

Edited by Jaclyn Reuter
Cover Design by Danijela Mijailovic
Formatting by Tapioca Press

ISBN: 978-1-7378369-0-2 (Paperback)
ISBN: 978-1-7378369-1-9 (EBook)

Publisher email address: mkitsios8@gmail.com
Printed by Maria Kitsios, in the United States of America.
First printing edition 2021

Dedicated to my dear father.
I hope your transition was smooth and painless.
Thank you for giving me life,
for supporting and encouraging me,
for loving me unconditionally on this path.
I will always love and miss you—
until we reunite.
I find strength in feeling your presence protecting me still.

INTRODUCTION

The Crown Chakra

According to the Vedas (ancient Indian sacred texts), the physical body is composed of seven main energy or vortex centers called chakras. Chakra is the Sanskrit word for wheel. The seven main chakras run along the spine-beginning from the root and ending with the crown chakra.

1. Root
2. Sacral
3. Solar plexus
4. Heart
5. Throat
6. Third eye
7. Crown

Each chakra has a different color, element, sound, mantra, function, location, major organ, and association. The flow or blockage/imbalance of subtle energy in each chakra determines the health or disease of the individual body.

This book is the first of a series of seven poetry books. Each book is composed of poems which discuss matters of one specific chakra.

In yoga practice, we usually begin from the root chakra and elevate to the crown chakra. However, I decided to start with the crown chakra and work my way downwards. I do this in order to honor all who have physically left this world, yet are still present and connected to us. It is the last and highest of the chakras, the one most associated with the metaphysical, spiritual realm.

Crown Chakra information:
Sanskrit name: Sahasrara
Color: Violet, gold, and white
Element: Thought and consciousness
Sound: Om
Mantra: "I Know"
Practice: Sitting meditation
Function: Understanding
Location: Top of the head
Organ: Cerebral cortex and the central nervous system
Associations: Faith, courage, spirituality, connection, and selflessness
Dysfunctions when imbalanced: Depression, apathy, confusion, insomnia,
sensitivity to light and sound, memory loss, boredom, and mental disorders.

1. EXCAVATION OF SPIRIT

We travel through lifetimes
in search of knowledge, experience, truth, essence of being.
On the walk towards different paths
we sometimes sit to rest.
We find a stranger sitting beside us
and so, we exchange bliss
for a few, fleeting moments
only to get up again
and walk our separate roads.
Those which lead back home
are always taken in solitude.
Maybe we gain a helping hand on steep and rocky terrain
or we must find the courage to climb alone.
Remain grateful for the help.
Remain proud of your bravery.
Remain unattached to the journey
and everything in it.
It is an illusion.
One which will vanish
in the blink of our eyes.
If we're lucky someone will be there
to close them for us.
They can even toss our ashes in the ocean
and tell tales of an identity which once inhabited the Earth
in our form and name.
It won't matter either way.
For we are simply wanderers,
whether lonely or crowded.

Solitary wanderers lost in an unknown place,
wondering why we are here
and what crazy desire urged us
to begin this long and strenuous excavation of spirit.
Remain grateful to those who helped you bury old ways.
Remain grateful for those who understood the uniqueness in you.
And always wish them well.

2. RETURN HOME

The traveler,
the world explorer
understands life.
With curiosity and openness
he wanders to foreign lands.
Yet amongst the joy
he knows
one day he will say goodbye-
bittersweet farewells
whispered to strangers
who became friends
separating again now.

The ultimate traveling experience
is to and from this realm.
Let's understand life this way.
We are only here in passing—
until the trip comes to an end
and we must return home.
Let's travel lightly.

3. LEAVE IT ALL BEHIND

When we lose someone we love,
our life completely changes.
Death causes us to think of non-attachment—
a concept Buddha spoke often about.
We can't even be attached to this plane of existence
for one day we will leave it.
Yet, no one ever teaches us how
to practice non-attachment.
No one ever talks about the importance of it.
We all just act like we'll be here forever.
But the raw Truth is
one day we will leave behind everything,
everyone we love.

4. OXYTOCIN CALCULATIONS

Our oxytocin levels escalated again.
So I find myself lost
in the Universe behind your eyes,
dwelling cheerfully
in the smooth curves around your lips.
Breathing life into each other—
consumed in the peace, the passion, the lust,
the rare connection.
I tell myself I'm in trouble
or in love.

Same difference.

But I know I am safe.
For as long as anything lasts
within a fleeting existence,
I want to be
fully captivated in this
calculated miracle—
drowning in the deepest
and most expansive
waters of Consciousness.
And if life forces us to separate
as two particles
split, change, evolve,
I will let go with grace
knowing I have lived
a bond as unique as each sunset.

I will not be bitter or angry,
only grateful
and bid farewell with a smile.
For who can say he glanced
upon himself
in eyes of another
without feeling beauty's embrace?
It could be the oxytocin.
Maybe it hasn't worn off yet.
Or maybe,
just maybe
I am happy here.

5. THE DIVINE WITHIN

Every one of us seeks to understand
what brought us into existence.
We seek to know the Creator.
That is the most sought after truth,
enigma, life mystery.
So we embark on journeys
of religious study or
spiritual revelation—
forgetting the simplest of truths.
Man and woman come together
and through love expressed,
a being is brought
into this physical realm.
Before we can look beyond this form of creation,
we need to understand it.
For we, humans, are Creators.
We are Creators of love
and through love
we create.
This is the cycle of life
and it is impossible to live
away from this natural cycle.
So feel the Divine within!

6. GODDESS

I am a humble Goddess.

7. REASON

We are here to face why we need to be here—
to experience the lessons we must learn in this realm
in order to grow
into the abundant potential of the Universe within—
the state always present in each of us.

8. WE ARE THE SOURCE

We are the Source we come from;
the place we will return to one day.

9. BRING ME WISDOM

It can be painful to let go
of youth,
but as the days pass
I become wiser,
more gentle and loving.
So let the years come and go.
Wisdom is all I want to hold.
Time,
bring me the will to know!

10. ALL KNOWING WISDOM

One day, all this will be
just a moment in time.
Then you'll come to see
there's nothing you can't survive.

And as the seasons change
with the cycles of the world
you'll realize that this life
constantly unfolds.
It unfolds like a rose
with petals exposed.
Breathes into our being;
wisdom of all that knows.

So don't let an instant
harm your spirit.
One day, this lesson will be learned
and time will reveal it.

11. LIFE REVEALED

What if life were
not at all as it seemed
and all that lay before us
was an ocean full of dream?

What if instead of falling into bed
and waking up abruptly
we lived a false illusion
which proved itself subtly?

What if all we ever knew
was a lie within itself?
Would that revelation change our beliefs
and let the Truth prevail?

Would it unmask the secrets
which lay locked within a cage
or make us full of fury,
bring us close to rage?

Would we be more miserable
than a mother who's lost her child
or free as an untamed animal
found within the wild?

12. UNDERSTANDING

Observing the human mind, behavior, and constitution.
The study of the spirit.
Study of consciousness.

Understanding the mind,
understanding the spirit,
understanding the body.

When we see the connection between these three,
we begin to discover the depth of existence.
Sharing in the knowledge of this depth is Love.

13. EXPERIENCE IS A TEACHER

Experience is the greatest teacher.
It helps the soul advance and grow.
Only through adventure can we truly know
this elusive concept called "Self."
Don't be afraid to live.
Live freely and fearlessly like a child.
Dance wildly in the street.
Give your smile and heart to the world.

14. OPENING PORTALS

I'm closing the gates,
but I'm opening portals.
DIVINITY communicating
with us, mortals.
A street sign
is enough to inspire
when you're made of
water and fire.
Stay humble
within all your desires.
Use this life you are given
to elevate the Self and serve others.
Let us take time
to sit and honor
the Creator's presence
with ours.

15. EMBODIMENT

In a moment of reading about
spirituality and enlightenment,
someone came to me in need of
comfort, support, and affection.
That is when I closed my book
and put my teachings into practice.
Only a fool would miss
such an opportunity to share.
It is not enough to obtain knowledge.
Through awareness,
we must embody it as well.

16. FRUITS OF THOUGHT

I love to indulge in the feast of my mind.
There, I find gratification and sadness combined.
There, in the fruits of my thought,
I stare at the true essence of humanity.

17. GREAT THINKERS

It is of no coincidence
the greatest thinkers in history
all regarded simplicity and humbleness
as the greatest possessions.

18. PHILOSOPHER'S MIND

The role of the seeker of truth,
that of the philosophical
and working mind
is to question everything.
Question all that is believed to be true.
Even our senses
and perception of daily reality
is skewed.
There are other mammals
which have higher auditory
and visual capacity than us.
So the human ear and the human eye
aren't superior from a scientific standpoint.
Therefore,
it is utter ignorance to believe
everything we hear or see.
Undiscovered realms await us.
If only we rise from the content
we experience in comfort
and develop the courage for exploration.
Bring back the philosopher—
the one who doesn't sleep
for his urge to know
is overpowering.
A deep yearning to know the truth of all things.
It is this desire that breathes life
into his being.

19. PHILOSOPHER'S CONCLUSION

The philosopher's greatest conclusion:
Meditation is the only way to understand existence
and answer life's deepest questions.
Anything you experience there,
is all there is.

20. IF IT BE LIVED SO

How does man live
without passion in his heart?
No dream has ever come
without it being sought.

How does man live
with hatred in his soul?
Love is but a seed—
nurtured to fruit it will grow.

How does man live
when trusting in a lie?
Honesty is the only home
for knowledge to reside.

How does man live
fearing death so?
To fear death is to dread life
for all is an unknown.

How does man live
without dignity in his word?
Deception has only
deception lured.

How does man live
without desiring to grow?
Life is but a hell if it be lived so.

21. NOTHINGNESS

Everything is nothing.
We are nothing.
Just an illusion
dreamt up and created
by Source—
manifested in this realm
which we perceive as reality.
We are specks
of all encompassing energy.
Meeting itself again and again
through any connection we make.
Connection with nature,
connection with one another.

22. NON-ATTACHMENT LIFE

Remain unattached.
This one simple statement is the only way to live a happy life.
The Buddhists have been teaching non-attachment for centuries.
This philosophy has so much depth, yet is so simple.
I find the simplest things are always the deepest.

If you hold your breath too long, you suffocate yourself.
Don't be attached to the day
because the sun sets into a new one.
Or to physical objects with sentimental value
because they may break.
Let go of beliefs which no longer serve you.
Don't be attached to desired outcomes
or images you have of your future,
interactions with others
because you both grow,
whether together or apart,
or your looks because you're aging too.

Everything is in constant change.
It is the principle of nature.
Energy constantly flows.
So flow with it.
Trust the Divine flow.
Go with the flow.

23. LOVELY PATH

Visions of a tiny boy
running wild in the park.
A pooch is jumping around
with his innocent bark.
The sun is shining bright
and the wind is passing by.
This lovely path is right
and it is mine,
it is mine!

Oh, the Universe knows best—
the purpose of it all.
The passion in your heart
and the desire of your soul.

Scents of flowers' pollen,
love is in the air.
The horses' sweet manure
and their flawless dare.
The freshly watered grass
staring at the sky.
This lovely path I pass
and it is mine,
it is mine!

Oh, the Universe knows best
the purpose of it all.
The passion in your heart

and the desire of your soul.

This is how life is
every single day
when you hold onto your passion
and throw your fears away!
It is a summer walk
through the gorgeous park.
An exciting and endless journey
to courageously embark.

24. SPIRITUAL REVOLUTION

I want to start a revolution.
Evolution!
A revolution of the spirit.
One where people discuss the metaphysical
as they talk about the weather
and other insignificant things of a temporary nature.
I think that our work as living entities is to revolt against
the mundane
and delve deep into existence, itself.
That is our only purpose here in this realm—
to unravel the layers of conditioning and free our spirit
from the chains of the delusion
that we are present for no purpose at all.
Delve into and embrace your deepest nature,
my beautiful friends!
This body, this life, this moment is temporary and fleeting,
but YOU,
your SELF is eternal!
Infinite and abundant is what you are!
Live free from the conditionings which tell you otherwise.

25. BAPTISM

What is within a name?
What can be described and labeled
or fit within a tiny box of adjectives
given by man unstable?

What wisdom and what life?
What can sounds describe?

With what words can hurt
or ecstasy be
thoroughly understood
when no one is standing
where you stood?

What is within a name?
What fragments of time
can be captured in fleeting
echoes of the voice?
With same pleasure
can others rejoice?

Where can all thoughts be told?
Who is there to understand them
when the poet has grown old?
What is within a name?
What beauty and what pain?
How can this realm eternity hold
in moments of death and disdain?

26. WHAT ARE WE IN THE END?

What are we in the end?
This system which governs us—
maybe it knows.
All the years
we spent on desks
and useless jobs.
All those
daily, heavy steps
we take, going nowhere,
towards a future
already controlled
by our inevitable death.
Who can tell us
what we're doing here?
In the few years
we're blessed
to exist in this world.
What are we in the end?
Maybe simply
flesh and bones
with uncleansed blood
that flows?
Or maybe the mind
that torments us?
Maybe we're just loneliness.
But who can you express
all this to?
And what could he comprehend?

Which crazy being
has ever been taken seriously
and who his logic could understand?
What are we in the end?
Beyond the labels
others place upon us?
What meaning is there
in the last breath
before a trigger is pulled?

27. TRUST IN THE JOURNEY

Stop and smell the flowers.
Feel the freedom of the butterflies.
Look into the eyes of the dogs which pass.
Embrace the silence in the morning rise.

Talk with each other as if you are talking with God.
Place your feet on Mother Earth.
Let the ocean soak your hair.
Hug another as you would a vulnerable child.

Give your smile to people who seem troubled.
Hold the door for those behind you.
Be present in the Now.
Life is this moment.

Do not be fooled by your mind.
Do not stay stuck in your past
and do not worry about your future.
Trust in the journey to Source.

28. SPIRIT COMPREHENDS

My surroundings speak to me.
They tell me of the subtle movement
of the leaves—
green as they are richly hanging off
of branches this spring afternoon.
The soft and invisible swaying
back and forth
mimicking the blood which flows through veins
each instant we live
unaware of these special occurrences
and miracles of life.
Undergoing changes.
Every breath exhaled
and new life inhaled in all of existence.
Becoming aware that life is fragile,
yet endless—
in beauty and travesty.
Knowing and understanding
with the instinctual mind
that some day
this body will cease to exist.
Logic cannot fully grasp such a reality.
But spirit comprehends.
There is no beginning and no end.
All which exists and ever existed
is change.

29. CONNECTING THE STARS

Connecting the stars
and admiring them.
So scattered and bright,
endless as I am.

Counting the stars
tonight in the darkened sky,
I realize I am nothing
more than a mere sigh.

Connecting the stars
and absorbing their essence,
makes me recall
my own eternal presence.

30. DRIFTING OF CLOUDS

Watch the clouds drift away.
They are like the people in our lives.
Aren't they?
Coming and going.
Staying only for a bit so we can admire them.
Some days are filled with clear sky.
And, almost like a mirror,
we are able to better reflect upon ourselves.
Nature teaches us more about life
than any other teacher ever could.

31. MOUNTAINS

The mountains look down
upon me
and for the first time
I appreciate
being looked down upon.

32. SNOWFLAKES

I like to look at snowflakes
the way I see all individual beings.
Falling from the sky as tiny specks
only to combine with one another
bit by bit,
yet so much so
in forming mountains
of snow.

A collective of the purest white
piling on each other
in the greatest reflection
of light.

I like to look upon snowflakes
as individual parts of the grand sublime.
All has its purpose
within the Divine.

I like to admire the beauty
of everything around me
and in this place of gratitude
I vow to always be.

I vow to remain present
to the breathtaking views of nature's art.
Those resembling
the light within my heart.

33 · MESSENGERS

The birds carry with them
many memories
of which they can't recall.
But they carry them in their stride.
Like the wind carries
aromas of the beloved
and longings of the lonely.
The birds share many secrets
with the rest of us
as we share them with our silence.

34. FEATHERS OF A BIRD'S CORPSE LIE

Feathers of a bird's corpse lie
along the path which I passed
and the wind blew them fiercely by.
Nature knows not the difference
between life lived and life taken.
The elements continue on
as they have before.
It's a cycle
that changes with the seasons.
This life concludes
the same as it began.
The ego may deceive you
of your own significance.
But trust me:
you too shall be forgotten.
I see no greater beauty
than to live
and be forgotten.
To know that all I give
was given in each moment
for that moment
and nothing more.

35. CONSTANT STATE OF FLUX

It's difficult to slow down and see things
how they are
because once you get a glimpse of them,
they change.
Being in a meditative state shows us
it takes a lot of acceptance to simply be.
Being is non attachment.
This is why if we're not excited, we are bored.
We constantly seek out
something,
anything
to prevent us from being present, still, aware
of the constant state of flux.

36. NATURAL PROCESS

To understand ourselves
we must first look to
and understand
the natural process of all things.
We must look to understand
the deepest workings
of the natural world.
The chaotic and always changing
nature of the Universe, itself.

37. ENHANCED SENSES

I can feel the sound of the waves
brush against my bare feet
and I can see the scent of the ocean's salt
seep into my skin.
I taste the sun's embrace with my fingers
and hear the colors of the horizon
calling out to me.
My senses are enhanced and endless.
Nature's beauty brings me back
to my deepest level of being
and I am consumed by stillness.

38. NEVER TRULY ALONE

When we learn to communicate and connect with energy,
we are never truly alone.
Nature is better to connect with than most humans.
Humans are so fearful, so guarded.
Nature openly gives and receives love.

39. BREATH

Breath and Intention—
both determine the flow of your life.

40. ACHIEVEMENT

To earn money:
we work.
To build muscle:
we exercise.
To learn:
we observe.
To teach:
we show.

Every achievement requires some form of action to be taken.
The greatest accomplishment is to grow as a spirit; to expand.
Since spiritual growth is the ultimate purpose of existence,
shouldn't we be meditating?
What are we doing to evolve spiritually?

41. LIFE GOALS

When we think of life goals,
oftentimes we contemplate
the material aspect—
things we aspire to obtain
outside of ourselves.
Whether they be a dream home,
a lifelong partnership,
a book of poetry,
a family,
or flourishing career.
Although I too find myself
setting such goals,
my ultimate goal is to become a buddha,
an enlightened one.
To reach such a state
and share it with the world.
Life is the greatest opportunity given to us
to elevate our spirit.
Focusing on such a goal makes all the rest
seem relatively insignificant.

42. ENLIGHTEN

Truth is never harsh.
Your judgement might make it seem so.
Upon hearing it for the first moment
it might feel heavy.
Simply because it tears down your ego.
But if you take time to think about it,
truth is always light!

43. BECOME AWARE

Meditation.
The way to form positive thoughts is
to first become aware of the negative ones.
It is a word,
an affirmation,
a vibration
which emits a certain frequency
and attracts things,
situations,
and people to you.
Consciousness is listening
to your intention and beliefs.
Make sure you're manifesting
an abundant life.

44. PRAISE YOU

Energy of this abundant and expansive Universe!
I praise the beauty of you;
for you exist within me
and I am a speck
of you,
Eternal Existence!
You are the Creator
and the creation.
Manifest into all beings,
all spaces,
and forms.
I praise you,
dearest Love.
Grateful for I see you
in all the beauty of the world
whether subtle or obvious.
Glimpses of you appear
to the aware I.

45. GREAT SPIRIT

Dear Great Spirit,
I ask for the strength to endure
all of the uphill on this journey.
I am grateful for the moments of rest
in which I slow down and connect with you
through stillness and silence
and prayer.
May your guidance follow me
through all my adventures
and lead me into the abyss of growth.
May your love fill my being
with light of a thousand stars.
May I always have the courage
to speak of your truth
and be the vessel of your purpose.
My dearest Source,
thank you for being
my mother, my father,
my sister, my brother,
my greatest friend.
I am grateful for your daily miracles
and the support you give me
every moment of my life.
I am grateful for existence;
sacred opportunity to evolve.

If ever I lose my way to you,
please gently bring me back

to the beauty and light of my heart.
For love resides in this wounded place.
I touch the ground every day
in great humbleness
and admiration.
Through the roots of my ancestors
I plant my feet and ground myself.
Only then am I able to reach
the abundant heights
of which we are all capable.
May I be an embodiment of compassion
especially in moments when
my ego is bruised.
May the harshness of this world
never touch my spirit.

I love you, Creator.
I will honor you in my words, actions,
and presence.
Love and Light,
Your Vessel of Truth.

46. HEALTHY LIFE

If we pay close attention we see
our mood is greatly affected by our physical body.
If we walk around with unreleased stress
which we aren't consciously aware of,
we will start to feel unhappy emotionally as well.
This is why the trilogy is important:
mind, body, soul.
Each affects the other tremendously.
So take care of all aspects of yourself to lead a healthy life.

47. WE CARRY WITH US

We carry with us
all the moments in time
which brought joy to our hearts.
Like the feathers of a bird,
we carry burdens of heartache.
Like skin of a snake
we carry traces of fingers
which ran through our bodies.
We carry sighs and yearnings.
We carry laughter and cries.
We carry them
until the day comes
when we release them all
into the Universe.
We release them in prayer,
offering thanks to existence for our experience.
We release all we once carried
and held onto tightly
because we know
past no longer suits us,
it no longer fits who we are.
And so, each day
we are born anew.
For we are not defined
by the labels, scars, or memories
of times long gone.
Each day brings with it
possibility and abundance.

48. COSMIC DANCE

No more safety nets
or comfort pillows
left to lean on.
I no longer entertain
limiting thoughts about myself.
Now I trust in my strength.
I speak to myself
as I would to any being I love.
"It is time, babygirl.
Move ahead,
unafraid
into your greatness.
Elevate
to your High Self.
It is time, my Queen."

Love yourself.
Every moment be kind to yourself.
Speak nicely to your mind,
meditate and connect
with your soul to the Divine.

Treat your body well and build it to be strong,
relentless like you.
Sit in meditation and connect your body to your mind
using the all-powerful breath!
Breath is life.

When we are loving to ourselves
we can be more loving to one another.
So, I cultivate myself
and re-experience myself
a thousand times in passing
as the sacred Creator does
through me.
A cosmic dance back
to remembrance of who we are.
A message we are here to share with the world.

49. CLEANSE OUR SOUL

We must dust negativity off our mind
the way we dust dirt off our shelves.
We must rid of our trauma
the way we sweep our floors.
It is the way
to be kind to ourselves.
So let us mop away our past
and cleanse our soul.

50. MAKE LOVE WITH
YOUR SELF

When was the last time you made love with yourself?
And I don't mean by tugging at your genitalia
until you reach physical pleasure.
(Everyone seems to find time to do that.)
I mean sat with yourself,
put your mind aside,
embraced your own presence and stillness.
Meditation is in essence a making love to your own being.
Nothing is more important than breathing love into yourself.
Push aside the bully in you—
the one who judges and worries constantly.
Push him aside and come into contact with your Higher Self.
The God in you is yearning for your attention.
Be present with Him.
It is the only way to be blissful.

51. NURTURING TOUCH

We don't caress each other or ourselves much.
Have you noticed?
As a baby,
everyone cuddles and caresses us.
We receive so much of this love.
Yet at some age,
we universally decide
"That's not appropriate.
You're too old to be caressed."
Physical touch becomes so sexualized and taboo.
But the yearning within us for loving touch never subsides.
So many studies have proven how essential it is
for a human's psychological state.
We become cut off from a crucial need and isolated from love—
a physiological need that seems odd to the majority.
It is so overlooked.
We don't even caress or give that nurturing touch to ourselves.
Even then, we think of masturbation.
But it doesn't have to be in that form.
Give yourself a caress with intent of sending pure love.

52. I WANT HER

I want to share my life with Love.
Get up every morning and make love to her.
Feel her in my heart with every beat.
Embrace her in every hug I give.
Recognize her behind every smile.
Receive her in strangers' kindness.
I want her to see me in naked aloneness
and be forever present, near me.
Yes, my partner shall be Love!

53. LETTING GO

Learning how to let go takes practice.
But when you're absolutely forced to,
do it gracefully and with compassion.
Letting go can sometimes be the greatest act of love.

54. STAND TALL

Constant flow
of holding on
and letting go.
Constant struggle
to be found
among the peaceful
and the wild.
Yin and yang
are part of one
and part of all.
As we rise
and as we fall,
Source guides us
to stand tall.

55. I BELONG

I belong to the expansive sky,
to the stars,
to the heavens above.
I belong to the mountains,
to the horizon,
to abundance and Love.

I belong to the sun,
to the light,
to the desert heat.
I belong to the fire,
to burning desire,
to nature's beat.

I am vulnerable,
but strong.
If I'm unbendable
I don't last long.

I belong to the ocean,
to the rivers and streams,
to the valleys down low.
I belong to the waterfalls,
to the lakes and the seas,
to the current flow.

I am vulnerable,
but adaptable too.

Like water I change form
from ice to dew.

I belong to the forest,
to the trees and the trails,
to the wild plants and Earth.
I belong to the dirt,
to the soil,
to the Mother that gave me birth.

56. SYMBOL OF MY TRIBE

A symbol of my tribe—
healers who work with
elements of Love and Light.
Wear the grey highlights with pride
and let the tribe unite!
Casting magical spells
with the all-powerful "Eye".
Words hold the key
to elevating high.
Create in this abundant Universe.
All that is, is in the I.

57. CEREMONY

In times of ceremony,
the Self and the collective
integrate.
In the stillness and silence
found within,
we come to be
the essence of our truest nature.
Nature is Love.
Amidst the chaos
and the peace.
Acceptance of all which passed,
that which is present,
and the infinite possibility
to be experienced.

The eternal opportunity
to reinvent ourselves
through the cycles of inhalation,
exhalation.
Holding on,
letting go.
We surrender
to the power in forgiveness.
It is done effortlessly
as we sit with the wisdom
and compassion
of the heart.

58. PSYCHEDELIC

Meditation, itself, is a psychedelic.

59. THE HIGHS

The best highs are those which
aren't a result of any substance intake.
Those highs brought about naturally,
those are the highs worth living for.

60. MOST HIGH

The connection, strength, beauty and peace
which exists in the depths of a single tree
are far beyond any ever experienced
when dealing with humanity.
Nature is therapeutic for the mind and heart.
Make sure to sit with yourself
in places untouched by human imperfection.
Sit with yourself and realize
your own Divine nature.
The most High exists within your heart.
Everything you've ever wanted is within you.
Never look for it outside of yourself.

61. LOWS AND HIGHS

Embrace where you are.
Experience every emotion you feel.
Fully live it out and express it.
There's nothing wrong with that.
Who's to say we need to be happy all the time?
That's not possible in human experience.
What is possible is awareness.
As long as you're aware
of the impermanence of your present emotional state
(and all others that are to follow)
you're living in a realistic way.
Human experience is made up of lows and highs.
Stop trying to deny yourselves the lows.
They too are beautiful.
Your life is this moment.
During unpleasant moments,
moments of difficulty, stress or fatigue
we desire to speed up time—
to leave the current state and enter another,
not realizing that this is life.
This and every moment,
pleasant or unpleasant.

62. WE ARE MANIFESTING

We Are Manifesting.
Three very powerful words.
Each day we manifest.
We attract into our lives
experiences which will either elevate us into abundance
or bring us down.
We manifest experience our soul has been preparing for.
Every day up to Now has been
a preparation for purpose's manifestation.
Our lives are a constant teaching
for the next level of our greatness.
And somehow in the midst of everything I manifested you—
to look into my third eye and show me my vision.
Opening that eye up to the heavens of the crown
and making my dreams a tangible reality.
We are who we surround ourselves with
and we are better when we exist in oneness.

63. HUMAN MANIFESTATION

I'm touching the human manifestation of your soul.

64. MANIFESTED

We manifested one another in a Universe where
the mind and heart bring us abundance!

65. REMEMBRANCE

We are Love manifested in human form.
Life's journey is a remembrance of this Truth.
Once we come to this wisdom,
we are only then fully capable of Divine experience.
In this realm,
we can easily stray from our true nature and become distracted
with the mundane and practical.
But that is not what this temporary life is about.
My flesh, my identity will fade away one day.
You will no longer be able to touch my skin or hear my voice.
My essence will continue on.
And this is the part of me, the Love of me,
which I will continue to share with the world.

66. WE ARE ALL

We are all.
All of it.
The shadow and the Light
combined.
We are what we see in others.
See the beauty in each other.

67. CREATE MAGIC

We are alchemists
working with the elements:
Earth, Metal, Water, Wood, Fire.
Let's consciously manifest
our heart's purpose
and soul's desire.

We are alchemists
awakening from a deep trance
and finally we're flowing
in sacred Cosmic dance.

We are alchemists
who blindly worked with energy.
Now we use our Magic
to create intention-ally.

We are alchemists
using our hands to feel,
our love to heal
and with every breath
we now choose
to embody our ideal.

We are alchemists
turning all we touch
into priceless gold.
Come to know this truth,

do not fear your power
and see the magic unfold.

68. MAGICIANS IN THE NIGHT

Nocturnal creatures—
dangerously beautiful.
Dangerous for they are powerful.
Their nature lures you into mystery
and their gentleness intrigues you.
The wisdom in their calmness;
their appeal in the dark.
Seductively hypnotizing you
with their intense glance.
Casting magic spells
with their soft voice,
and the intention in their words.
Words which
echo in your dreams
and consume your waking thoughts.
Nocturnal, seductive, intense, powerful,
gentle, intentional and wise—
magicians in the night.

69. MAGIC WAND

The mind is powerful.
The power it holds to change your reality
is beyond imaginable.
Yet, once we begin to imagine it,
we start to use it
as a magic wand of sorts.
Only then do we grow
into who we essentially are.

70. GREATER

You are greater than you can imagine.
You are greater than your biggest passion.
You are greater than your protective gear.
You are greater than your strongest fear.
You are greater than your ego fakes.
You are greater than your mistakes.
You are greater than your limiting beliefs.
You are greater than your mind deceives.
See, discover, accept, and take in
the greatness that's within.

71. STRIVE

Mediocrity is no longer for me.
Mediocre discipline,
mediocre mentality,
mediocre physique,
mediocre relationship to others and to Self
no longer intrigues me.
The flame within me
pushes me to the limit
to reach my full potential
of Love, Light, Strength.
I strive to constantly elevate and evolve.
Then I am able to embody my purpose of guiding others.
That is the reason I am here in this body.
The reason I was given this opportunity to live.
Excellence is what I strive for
in all my actions
and interactions.
Godliness is what I am.
So, I no longer have an interest in limiting myself.
I deserve more than a mere, flimsy mediocre
and I give more love than just enough to me.
I am more than that
and so are each one of you.

72. MEDITATIVE PROCESS

The first step
is to rid yourself of all distraction
(put the phone on silent and away from you,
turn the lights down low, sit or lay down).
Being present is the initial stage to meditation.
Sit with yourself in silence and stillness.
Turn inward.
Focus on any point in your body
which is calling you for love.
It could be a part that's achy or tense
or simply one you feel heaviness in.
These uneasy sensations are indicators
that you have energetic blocks in that specific chakra.
So focus on one specific area to begin with.
Feel it with your mind and then place your hand upon it.
Is it throbbing and overstimulated?
Or very faint and cold?
Whatever the case may be,
let your intention be to send love and healing to the area
through the palm of your hand.
Speak kind affirmations within your mind to nurture it.
Focusing on what is going on internally
is very important in meditation.
How can we truly know ourselves or anyone else
unless we tune into the energetic realm?
This is the deepest level of wisdom.
Yet, we foolishly spend our time stuck in the mind,
neglecting our wholesome being.

73. LABYRINTH

If you're avoiding time with yourself
it's only because you're running away from
unresolved pain and emotion
that remains dormant
in your subconscious mind.
It is still there.
The weight of it is pressing heavily
on your life.
Whatever we resist persists.
The only way out is in and through.
So let's walk our way out of the matrix
into the Love and Light of our Higher Self.
Walk through courageously,
unafraid of what you might find
inside the dark labyrinth of your mind.
You are strong enough
to face those demons.

74. CHATTER

In a world where your mind is always talking to you, how can you listen to anyone else?

75. STILLING THE MIND

Stilling the mind is a daily practice,
a worthy journey through the abyss and darkness of the mind.
Only after traveling through that abyss
can we learn to ease it into stillness.
Befriending our shadow side helps us to keep it in check.
We must be resilient in the process though.
Otherwise, it will swallow us whole.
So if you find yourself in the abyss, continue pushing forward.
That is a current state of affairs.
I'll see you all on the other, brighter side!

76. OBSERVER

Live your life as an observer—
as an observer of situations and people around you,
especially an observer of your own fleeting thoughts.
Only then can you truly understand in depth.
We value action so much in this society that worships extroversion.
Although action is necessary,
observation is true wisdom.
Unattached,
sit back and observe.
Remain unattached to all.
Even this life is temporary.
Your body, your mind, your entire entity
besides your consciousness
will only exist for a few years.
It is your spirit which will return to Source.
And your spirit is the one observing;
thus growing through observation.
The deepest purpose for presence in this ever-changing reality.
Until one day,
Source urges us to return home.

77. ELEVATE TOGETHER

Let's elevate together.
Let's rip out the old, negative and outdated baggage of the past.
Let's finally get out of our own damn way.
Let's put an end to stress, useless and self-defeating thoughts,
fears and worries.
Let's rise above and cleanse ourselves of injustice
in this world and in our hearts!
Let's connect with our ancestors, our Universe, our home of love!
Let's honor those who passed by living the life we are blessed with.
Let's make the most of this elusive experience and create.
Let's move away from the mere human state
and embrace the collective.
Let's express our individuality
through the beauty we bring to the world.
Let's embody the godliness around us and within us.
Let's be our own shaman and one another's.
It is possible and it is necessary.

78. LOSING SLEEP

I'm losing sleep,
losing sleep
doing things I love.
But it's better than losing it,
staring at the wall.

79. INSOMNIAC

Those who can't sleep
stay up and dream.
The misfits,
the rebels,
and the outcasts,
the solitarily
ecstatic creatures.
They glance at the moon
and howl with the wolves.
Their lips fill
with words needing expression.
Those who can't sleep
stay up and dream.

80. IN PRAYER

Let my hands
turn all they touch to gold.
Let my heart spread Love
into the unknown.

Let my lips
speak only Truth,
Wisdom, and Light.
Let my eyes embrace
their powerful foresight.

Let my legs fall only
in times of prayer.
Let my will-power
make this world fairer.

Let my mind raise
collective consciousness.
Let my presence
be thus blessed.

81. PRAYER FOR ALL

May I send nurturing warmth and peaceful energy
to those struggling with ego and resentment.
May my wishes be heard by the Universe and all its beings.
May all the love I ever held, all the beauty I ever felt,
turn into a blessing that lands on the restless and hurt.
May this wish be enough to bring a balance to all who suffer
from a life filled with painful experience and loneliness.
May the healing ability I possess
be sent out to anyone fighting a battle too harsh for one to bear.
May all the positive that lives within me
be a guide to save those I love from enduring a cruel life path.

Namaste!
In this temporary form.
Namaste!
And we have nothing to divide.
Namaste!
Until we go back where we came from.
Namaste!
Back home.

82. AS THE DAYS GROW OLD

As the days grow old
I do so too at once.
The minutes going by
smiling back at us.

The years that seem like hours,
decades seem like days.
The darkened blacks
which are now grays.

Times I looked ahead
to those I now look back.
Plans I once had
to those which now I lack.

As the days grow old
I do so too at once.
The seconds going by,
ruthlessly surpassing us.

Mistakes made
with no second chance.
If I could go back,
to every song I'd dance.

Life passes us whether we are or aren't there.
The young at heart, but young not be.
Time seems thus unfair.

83. EMBEDDED

It is all written on our faces.
The heartbreak and the pain.
The moments of joy and ecstasy.
Wrinkles deeply embedded on our spirit;
scars left as markings on our body
indicating that we have lived.

84. ONE DAY, I, TOO, WILL DIE

I, too, one day will die
and my heart
will one day cease to beat.
I, too, one day will die
and my lungs
will have no air to breathe.
I, too, one day will go
into the unknown,
other realm.
I, too, one day will go
with spirit spread
like branch of elm.
I, too, one day will cease
to exist in the form
that I currently do.
I, too, one day will cease
so as I'm here
I wish to say to you:
When the day comes
that my presence
can only be felt
and never seen
with the naked eye,
know that I live on
in memory, in heart, in mind,
in destruction of time.
For my spirit is endless,
my spirit is Love, and it won't ever die!

85. IT IS ALL PASSED

The past cannot be relived.
You must close that door.
The past is not here;
it was a moment ago.
The past has come and gone
many times in your mind.
Yet, past it is not,
but memories in time.
The past has been set,
written in stone.
You can't unsee
all you've been shown.
The future is the same—
not worthy of thought.
It is not here
and the present it's not.
The future is far
unless that moment has passed.
Now it's your present
and soon will be your past.

86. PAST

The past was yesterday.
The past is today
and it will be tomorrow too.
For no time
in time shall not pass.
So make the memories
somehow last
in your mind
and in your heart.
Love and live each day anew
right from the start.

87. WHEN I PASS

I want you to pour the wine
and raise a glass,
celebrate my existence
when I pass.

Think of me as the marvelous clouds
in the sky,
the sound of nature in the distance
and never say goodbye.
It is all that is an I.

I am the soil that makes the land,
the water that always flows,
the beach's golden sand.
Work with the Earth and feel my hand.

Light a match and cast a flame,
feel the fire's heat
and let it burn.
I'll be its overturn.

And when you sit in a forest
in view of every tree
remember that its bark is me.
Oh, if only you could see!

I'll be rigid metal that holds a home,
the one that never bends.

The Universe and I are friends.
Its memory never forgets.

So, please pour the wine
and raise a glass,
celebrate my existence
when I pass.

Think of me as energy
which never dies.
For I am nature in its eyes
and spare me your goodbyes!

88. ONCE UPON A TIME

The stories frightened us
and we would hide underneath our pillows.
Magically, the ghosts disappeared after.
Things were easy back then.
What happened only happened in the moment.
It was gone the next.
We constantly explored the world.
Nothing hurt us;
not even the bruises on both knees.
We were unbreakable
once upon a time.
Now we are broken for good
in our humbleness.
Once upon a time
the child hid eternally.
We yearn to return to that flesh again
in this life's game of hide and seek.

89. DISPERSE TIME ZONES

You think I could touch the stars
if I tried hard enough?
Could I hug the moon
and be one with the wind?
Do you think I have the strength
to freely wander the Earth
and disperse of time zones
created at birth?
How much power does it take
and who shall measure it so?
Who shall know such a gift
without letting this go?

90. JOURNEY TO SOURCE

The journey to Source
is taken alone.
It starts from the day we are physically born
into this human form.

A sort of recycling over and over.
Until we become acquainted with our inner lover.

Again and again.
It's a journey of laughter, of joy and of pain.
And all which is within this body
comes to remain.

Until the endless journey begins from the start.
And for the old spirit burdens the heart.

So, take me back and keep me, where I belong.
Universe, it is you I connected with all along.

So, let me go, bring me home.
I don't know if I want
to live as human anymore.

Take me to your abundance,
amongst the sky away.
Living on Earth is sorrow
on a fleeting day.

91. REACH YOU

I always follow you around—
behind your shadow every step,
but you never have enough time
to stop and notice I am there.
I am your every moment.
I am the now, the always, and the never.
You walk through open doors
without realizing I stand behind them—
naked, lustful, and awaiting your acknowledgment.
I am the mountain you climb,
I am the river in the forest,
I am the tree and its branches,
I am that snake in the distance,
hissing away.
That truck speeding,
recklessly out of control.
Who knows where I'll be hidden next
or what form I am willing to take.
Maybe I'll be the escalated heartbeat
or excess pills you take to sleep.
Maybe I'll be the pretty woman
dressed in red
walking down the street.
You may ignore me,
but I will continue to return
and alter your existence.
Sincerely,
Your Destiny.

92. LONGER

The longer we live,
the more we experience death.

93. WHO ARE YOU?

Who are you
when the lights dim down
and the curtains close?
Who are you
when you go inside
and lock the doors?

Who are you
when you unravel
all the corners of the mind?
Who are you
amongst the darkness
and the light?

Who are you
when you throw away
all of your useless layers?
Who are you
in your moans
and in your prayers?

Who are you
beyond conditioning
and years of training?
Who are you
when with the world
you stop comparing?

Who are you
beyond what others
label you to be?
Who are you
beyond the maya
of this illusory?

Who are you
the moment before
you let go of this life?
What thought is the last
to stay within your
weeping mind?

Who is it you struggle
to let go of as you leave?
What false identity
is left here to conceive?

The moment you let go of
everything you've known
the answer to this question
you are thus shown.

Death shows us Truths
life endlessly tries to conceal.
It is the inevitable
insight into what's real.

94. CHANGING FORM

Life is temporary and one day we'll have to let go
of all we see as reality.
Make space to think of your own transition from this form.
It is a very bittersweet truth to understand.
It humbles you and you're able to have
deep connection and sharing of
love with others.
Since we are human it's hard to not be attached
to any aspect of the human realm.
It's all just a constant flow of change and transformation.
Like energy never created nor destroyed,
but only changing form.

95. WE'RE ALL MADE OF CLAY

What difference does it make
to have lived at all?
We touch each other
mentally, spiritually, physically.
Yet, we're all made of clay
and that clay will melt
back to the Earth one day.

What difference does it make
to laugh, to cry, to play,
to work, to dance, to lay?

Any thought that has ever burdened
the crazy mind,
any emotion which has ever risen
and taken life inside.
All is meaningless
in the face of death
so, tell me a reason for which
life is worth living at all.

What difference does it make
to have lived at all?
We touch each other
mentally, spiritually, physically.
Yet, we're all made of clay
and that clay will melt
back to the Earth one day.

96. AS THE PREPARATIONS BEGIN

As the preparations begin
and the flowers are placed
please don't look upon me
as if I am erased.

Never before have I been so silent,
lacking a big smile,
so it may seem harsh today,
but please stay for a little while.

Greetings are welcomed here today.
Hellos may be better than goodbyes,
but please stay
for all that lives at some point dies.

I beg of you to not wear black
for all our days were bright.
Please don't hit rock bottom
for we had reached great height.

But most of all don't shed a tear
for it would drown my soul.
Immortality cannot be reached
although it was our goal.

You may think it irrelevant
to meet me here at all,
but I want you to take my hand

and talk me through my funeral.

97. BID FAREWELL

I will cease to exist.
In this form,
in this reality
I will no longer be present.
I realize this
not as an abstract thought
nor some philosophical
and poetic moment.
It was a clear awareness
of the inevitable.
Though it is difficult
for the ego to comprehend,
it is a humbling truth to acknowledge.
I have nothing to hold on to
when I understand that I will bid farewell
to my own body,
my own life one day.
There is an immense amount of freedom
within the fear of the unknown.
The freedom to be oneself unrestrained.

98. WE ARE LIMITLESS

Always add value to people's lives.
Our only purpose in human form is to grow spiritually.
And that can only be done by spreading our love
to those around us.
We are here for only a limited time,
but we are limitless.

99. WINGED THANATOS

When the day comes
and my soul can no longer take
the imprisonment of this body,
I want you to surrender
to the memories we've shared.

Surrender to the powerful
feelings we've felt.
Surrender to the lively moments
we've grown together
and then say farewell
to this body forever.

When the time arrives
and my soul eagerly pushes
to exit the flesh,
I'll give you an instant
to think back to the laughter
and give me your best.

Think back to the music,
the drinks, and the nights.
Think back to the talks
and the walks in the park.
Think back to the journeys
we dared to embark.

When the day comes

and my soul can no longer take
the body's restraint,
I'll give you my smile
and help you forget
all of the pain.

100. A SURFER'S DREAM

Mourning has many layers.
It is this complex and life-altering thing
no one prepares you for.
Not really, anyway.
They might say something like
"He's in a better place."
But no one mentions the details.
For instance,
you'll see everyone you love
cry and experience deep pain.
A sorrow you try to protect
your loved ones from
is now one you see in their eyes every day.
No one can prepare you for something like that.
To be there for someone else
while you are hurting too.
It is a lesson you learn
when grieving in a family.
The departed is missed by all who love him.
You come face to face with the truth of life
and the essence of it too.
All which are intense truths to be exposed to.
So, remember to ride the waves of sorrow.
That is something to be emphasized.
It all comes and goes like waves.
That is life, itself.
A surfer's dream.
Take care of yourself and be kind to your heart.

101. TAO

Do not cry for me,
my loves.
For when I die
I am not dead.
Do not hold sorrow
in your hearts.
It is the corpse
which lost its breath.
I live on and I transition
from this into the next,
changing forms
the way you change a dress.
Do not cry for me,
my loves.
Do not sink into despair.
There is nowhere I reside
for I live everywhere.
In the heart and in the mind
seek me if you dare,
I am the wind,
the little feather
flying in the air.
Do not cry for me,
my loves.
I lived my life as best one could.
I ran in forests with delight
and on mountaintops I stood.
You can find me in the light

and in the joys of laughter.
In the moon and in the night
it's you I will look after.
To be present and to hold
each other with compassion
is the purpose I've been told—
to love in highest fashion.
Do not cry for me,
my loves.
I travel freely even now.
My life has been a voyage
and it continues in the Tao.

102. TRAVEL THROUGH THE JOURNEY

As you travel to different continents
and foreign lands,
you meet a lot of different people.
From the beginning of your journey there
you know that your interaction with these people
is a temporary and brief encounter.
So you're able to easily say
goodbye when you part ways.
Yet, with people who live close to you
physically, mentally, and emotionally,
you become devastated
when they randomly leave.
If you change perception
and understand that life, itself, is
a temporary journey
then you can gracefully, wholeheartedly
accept when any person
(no matter how close)
leaves.
We will all eventually be
separated and reunited
by death anyways.

103. LEFT DYING ON THE ROAD

I saw a bird once
lying on the road.
It was shivering and shaking
left dying all alone.
There was no one around
and salvation was far gone.
For a struggling soul
nothing could be done.

I saw a bird once
left dying in the cold.
The image is engraved in memory
of sorrow's story left untold.
A voice was unspoken,
silence took its toll.
But what words can capture
grief's power over all?

I saw a bird once
losing the will to live.
Breath of life filled my lungs,
but life I couldn't give.
So I bowed my head in pain,
in honor of the dead
and with this poem I say
goodbyes I never said.

104. THE GRAVEYARD

Looking around the graveyard
you see what once were
smiles and dreams,
sorrows and fears.
You see lives and egos buried here
amongst the soil and the dirt.
Under the open sky and the green of trees.
Looking around the graveyard
you see the truth
of our human nature.
You see it planted
with the flowers,
like roots firm in the ground.
The inescapable,
undeniably humoristic irony.
The impermanence of it all.

Taking the last breath
feels exactly as the first.
The years go by
and emotions burst.
You smile, you laugh
you hurt, you cry,
you live, you learn
and then you die.
Taking the last breath
that seemed so far away—
you never saw it creeping up
right into today.
Suddenly all that mattered
fails to exist.
All you ever held
within your fist
has presently slipped
into mere space
with no expression
upon your face.
Taking the last breath,
your last breath.
You live your life
to reach your death.

106. SINCE YOU LEFT

Who could possibly ever hurt me now?
What miniscule and insignificant thing can ever bother me?
What words can possibly stab at me?
What actions can ever bring me sorrow?

Since you left
I lost the man who loved me unconditionally.
One of the only people who was always there.
So tell me what else can possibly sadden me,
knowing life is this unfair.

How can anything else have any sort of negative
impact on my heart?
It's a sort of apathy brought about by grief
and I felt it from the start.

This numbness to everything.
An apathy urging me
to go with the current flow of life.
Nothing really matters
or is powerful enough to bring me strife.

We are here one minute
viewing ourselves as important
because the ego deems us so.
Once that moment leaves,
the body is nothing anymore.

I do not say all this
with vibes of negativity.
I find it beautiful to have discovered
untapped strength in me.

By who and what
and when or how
can I be affected from
this world's injustices now?

I look to my heart
and thank you, dear dad.

You give me greater strength
than I've ever had.

I know it is you
each day and night
who's guiding me through
with your eternal light.

I love you forever
and miss you so.
I'll see you again
on a day unknown.

107. IF I KNEW

If I knew it was our last hug,
I would've held on a bit longer
and squeezed a little tighter
and told you "I love you"
just a little louder.
If I knew it was our last day laughing together,
I would've kept you here
a little longer
and made you laugh
just a little stronger.
If I knew it was our goodbye,
I would've held your hand
a little tighter,
I would've told you not to fear,
you're just elevating higher.
If I knew I wouldn't see you again
I would've looked into your eyes
a little deeper,
I would've hardened up
to fight against the reaper.

108. WE LOSE CLOSE ONES

We lose close ones.
We leave behind all those we love.
We constantly have to let go
of something,
of someone,
of a memory,
an idea,
a ghost,
a momentary feeling
that would only cause harm.
We let go of thoughts
which temporarily walk into the mind
and stroll about in search of food.
Life teaches us,
through his changing nature,
that we need to learn how to let go.
Death is the final teacher of
that same lesson
and we know how important it is.
We train for it logically all the time.
But, please,
don't think me weak
for crying over
such impermanence!

109. LOSSES

Death teaches us
how to let go,
just as every loss
in this life.
It teaches us
that we need to say goodbye
when the time is appropriate.
Every relationship that ends,
every friendship that's betrayed,
when we misplace our favorite books,
leave our phones in the train
while in a drunken state.
We always lose something
whether we expect to or not
and we then realize,
how well life sets the sheets
on our deathbed.

110. LOST

I don't think it's ever easy,
but you always have to let go—
of something you had,
someone you knew,
someone you were—
in order to grow.

I don't think it's ever easy,
but you must learn
to put aside your past,
put aside your losses,
push aside your fears,
and all of the things for which you yearn.

I don't think it's ever easy,
but nothing ever is—
nor can anything bring back
a lost spark,
a lost loved one,
a lost kiss.

III. ACCEPT IT

It takes courage
to sit with your pain
and look at it through
the mirror's reflection.
You are worthy
without needing perfection!

Tears drying on your face
as you hear a voice say
"You look so pretty when you cry."
I think of that any time
I cry for you.
You'd often joke
to make me laugh too.

Mourning is harsh,
but it takes strength
to hit the bag
instead of the bottle.
Escapism's many disguises
can be very subtle.
So many have lost themselves
in this dark place of sorrow.

I feel it too.
Every day I sit alone
and think of you.
Living a life unattached.

This one lesson
remains unmatched.

Face these truths
forging ahead.
Forget your ego,
nurture your heart instead.

Be kinder to you
when you're struggling through.
You need it then most.
"This all ends."
Accept that
in the realest sense.

~ACKNOWLEDGMENTS~

I want to express my gratitude for everyone who made this book possible.

Thank you to the Self-Publishing School and my coach, Barbara Hartzler. Your step-by-step guidance made the entire process much easier and enjoyable.

Thank you to my editor, Jaclyn Reuter, for her brilliant style and observant eye. Your recommendations made my voice clearer and words shine brighter.

Thank you to my formatter, Nola Li Barr, for her patience in answering all my questions. Your knowledgeable advice provided me with much needed clarity during the confusing process of publishing a book for the first time.

Thank you to my cover designer, Danijela Mijailovic. Your work is awesome and I thank you for bringing my vision to life in such a beautiful way.

My gratitude goes out to everyone who has been a part of my healing journey- my loving clients, my incredible colleagues, all my friends and teachers along the way. I am blessed to have encountered so many worthwhile beings along my life's path. Thank you for the exchange of knowledge, energy, and sharing of presence.

Thank you to my beautiful mother, Galatia Kitsios, for her constant love and support. I wouldn't be the person I am today if it weren't for the nurturing upbringing I received from you. Your incredible spirit and sensitive nature introduced me to the world of healing before I was even aware of it. Our connection is unique and we understand one another on the deepest levels.

Thank you to my dear brother, Spiro Kitsios, for being my very first friend in this world. I am eternally grateful for your protective nature and outstanding personality. You remind me to stay grounded and enjoy life fully.

Thank you to my sweet father, Ioannis Kitsios. I will forever cherish the memories we shared in this lifetime. The love between us is irreplaceable. We never doubted each other's love nor did we take it for granted. I feel your uplifting presence with me still.

Thank you to my lifelong friend, Maria Hristeas. You are the definition of a best friend. Your support, loyalty, honesty, and compassion have been a blessing for me.

Thank you to my soul sister, Aida Arias. I value our deep connection. Your humor and lightheartedness, loving and positive nature inspire me to remain humble as I evolve into my greatest potential. You and your family are family to me.

Thank you to my spiritual teacher, Carlos Alleyne. Your words are always few, deep, and powerful. I listen attentively to your guidance and I appreciate your presence.

Thank you to the magician archetype in my life, Raf. You are an endless well of wisdom, mental stimulation, and positive exchange. Time spent with you is valuable-two philosophers sitting across each other learning something new in discussion every time.

Thank you to my soul brother and medicine man-Stephen Charles. In nearly two decades of friendship, you always advise and look out for me, protect and respect me, and most of all understand me. I am grateful for the necessary tough love you give.

Thank you to my fellow healers and medicine women-Odalys Villanueva and Maya Martínez. You have given me much compassion, love and light during the darkest times. No words can express my everlasting gratitude for you.

Thank you to Mother Earth for grounding and centering me in the present.

Thank you to the enormous trees with their calming energy. Thank you for helping me breathe better and smile more often.

Thank you to the life-giving sun. Your fiery, bright rays energize me and feed my internal flame (solar plexus). Through your influence and intense, healing power I become more active in the pursuit of my dreams and fearlessly actualize them!

Thank you to water for balancing out my passionate nature. You remind me to listen to the subtle parts of myself-the whisper of my intuition, the gentleness of my feminine love, the softness in my sensuality, and the goddess in my sensitivity. You are my poetry and my forgiveness.

Thank you to all of the elements in nature and their interplay. Your sacred dance creates harmonious balance and is astonishing to watch!

Lastly, but never least, I am forever humbled in gratitude and in awe of the Divine. Thank you, dearest God, for your constant blessings. You are my Creator and I will continue to be your vessel of love and light within this worldly plane. The time I spend connecting with you in silent meditation is the most precious part of each day.

Namaste.

~ABOUT THE AUTHOR~

Maria Kitsios is a New York licensed massage therapist and Reiki master since 2013. Before dedicating her life to these healing modalities, she obtained a bachelor's degree in Behavioral Science. In 2021, she became a certified yoga instructor as well. Through many years of meditation, physical fitness, massage and energy work, she has discovered several truths about the mind/body/spirit connection on the deepest levels. She writes this book as an everyday guide, a reminder to live consciously and with purpose.

Join Maria's newsletter
and receive a free copy of the asanas guideline.

www.subscribepage.com/thejourneytosourceasanas

Instagram: @mkitsioslmt
Facebook: @Maria Kitsios, LMT